T0081471

CONTENTS

Cover photo © Robin Douglas-Home / Retna Ltd.

ISBN-13: 978-1-4234-0501-6
ISBN-10: 1-4234-0501-3

HAL•LEONARD
CORPORATION
7777 W. BLUEMOUND RD. P.O. BOX 13819 MILWAUKEE, WI 53213

Visit Hal Leonard Online at
www.halleonard.com

Come Fly With Me

Words by Sammy Cahn
Music by James Van Heusen

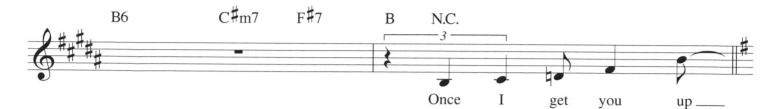

Once I get you up ___

Bridge

___ there, _____ where the air ___ is rar - i - fied, _

___ we'll _____ just glide, _____

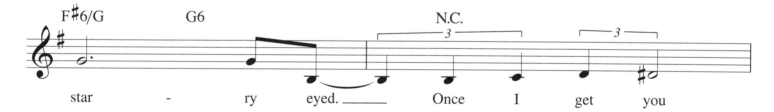

star - ry eyed. _____ Once I get you

up there, _____ I'll be hold - ing you _____ so near. _

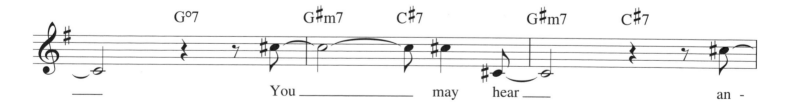

You _____ may hear ___ an -

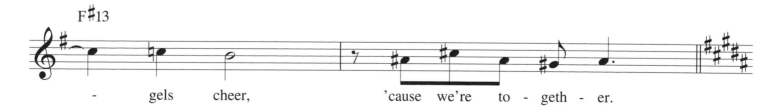

- gels cheer, 'cause we're to - geth - er.

Love and Marriage

Words by Sammy Cahn
Music by James Van Heusen

High Hopes

Words by Sammy Cahn
Music by James Van Heusen

dam.

Oops, there goes a

bil - lion kil - o - watt dam.

Interlude

Our prob - lem's

Outro-Chorus

just a toy __ bal-loon, they'll be burst - ing soon, they're just bound __ to go

pop! Oops, there goes an - oth - er prob - lem, ker -

plop. Oops, there goes an -

oth - er prob - lem, ker - plop. Ker - plop!

Love's Been Good to Me

Words and Music by Rod McKuen

My Way

English Words by Paul Anka
Original French Words by Gilles Thibault
Music by Jacques Revaux and Claude Francois

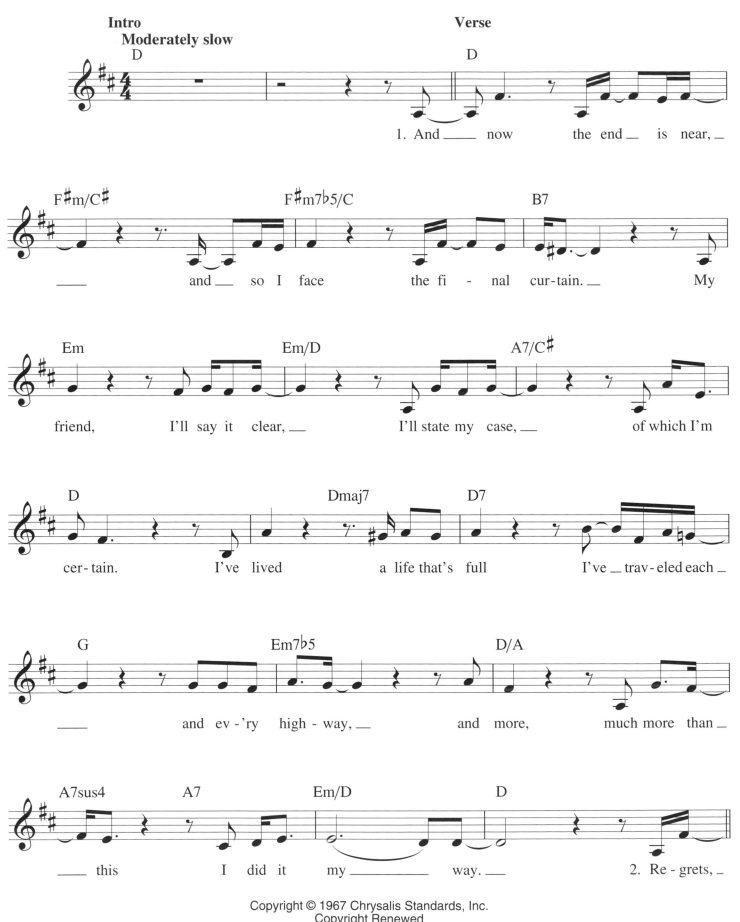

Strangers in the Night

Words by Charles Singleton and Eddie Snyder
Music by Bert Kaempfert

told me I must ___ have you. _____ Stran -

Bridge

Am7♭5

- gers in the night, two lone - ly peo - ple. We were stran -

A°7

- gers in the night up to the mo - ment when we

Gm7   Gm7♭5

said our first ___ hel - lo. ___ Lit - tle did we know, _

B♭/C   F/C   Dm   Gm7   C7sus4   C7

love was just a glance a - way, _ a warm em - brac - ing dance a - way, and

Verse
A tempo

F

2. ev - er since that night, we've been to - geth - er.

Fmaj7

Lov - ers at ___ first sight, _ in love for - ev - er.

Gm7   C9   Gm7   C9   F

It turned out so right for stran - gers in ___ the night. ___

23

(Love Is) The Tender Trap

Words by Sammy Cahn
Music by James Van Heusen

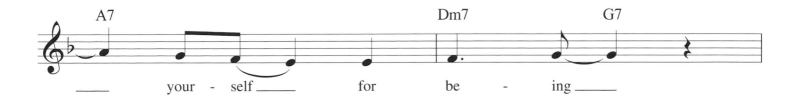

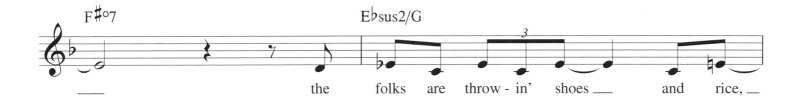

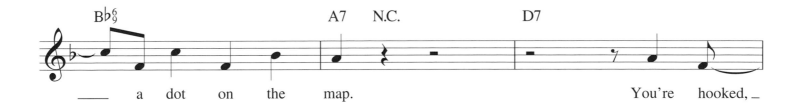

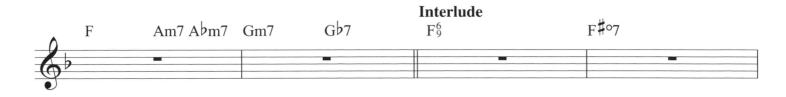

Young at Heart

Words by Carolyn Leigh
Music by Johnny Richards